23255

This book is to be returned on or before
the last date stamped below.

23255

TWENTIETH CENTURY
POSTERS

FERNAND MOURLOT

TWENTIETH CENTURY
POSTERS

CHAGALL/BRAQUE/PICASSO
DUFY/MATISSE/MIRÓ/LÉGER

WELLFLEET

Originally published copyright © 1959 by Andre Sauret as *Art in Posters*.
This edition published by arrangement with George Braziller, Inc.

Origination by Regent Publishing Services, Ltd.
Printed by Leefung-Asco Printers, Ltd.
Jacket design by Carmela Pereira
Manufactured in Hong Kong.
ISBN: 1-55521-385-5

The Wellfleet Press
110 Enterprise Avenue
Secaucus, NJ 07094

ALTHOUGH THE flood was probably not announced by means of posters, in order that it might come as a surprise, posters must have always existed : in antiquity, in the form of inscriptions; laws engraved in Greek; painted announcements of theatrical performances in Rome; wood-cuts in the Middle Ages; printed recruiting notices in the 17th and 18th centuries. Indeed, posters are to be found throughout history. They were rarely illustrated, however, before the invention of lithography, then of color lithography, made it possible to give practical expression in color to the illustrated poster.

From the Romantic period until the end of the century, certain artists made their career in the domain of commercial, travel, literary and theatrical advertising, and they produced an abundant number of posters, some of which are real masterpieces and still famous. Chéret, then Capiello, occupied important positions in a distinguished group of painters and designers, of which Lautrec was the undisputed leader, and which included Charlet, Raffet, Granville, Gavarni (here and there, Daumier and Manet) Steinlen, Ibels, Grün, Caran d'Ache, Bottini, Bonnard; all of whom contributed their talent and originality to production of lithographed posters.

About twenty years ago, at the same time that the com-

7

mercial poster was pursuing its successful career with such signatures as Cassandre, Paul Colin, Carlu, Loupot, Savignac, Jean Colin, Villemot, Morvan, etc. (we must apologize to the talented artists whose names are not on this list), with occasional reinforcements on the part of a few painters : Segonzac (Thérèse Dorny), Van Dongen (*Cecil* shoes, lip-stick), there appeared another form of illustrated poster by means of which painters announced their exhibitions. This flowering of 'colors combined in a certain order', which today brightens the windows of art galleries and antique dealers, is the subject of the following note.

Both as witnesses and, above all, as reflections of a time when advertising has become perennial, artists have left their ivory tower to exhibit in the market-place. One may ask why. According to the pessimist's explanation, an atmosphere of confusion and outbidding have made raising ones voice in order to make oneself heard by prospective purchasers a necessity. I believe, however, that they also have other, quite comprehensible, reasons for transforming the shop windows of certain sections of Paris into showcases.

The example of French State Museums, for instance, has undoubtedly been an incentive to painters to announce their exhibitions. Indeed, as far back as 1927, Jacques Jaujard, who at that time was assistant Director of Museums, had several remarkable posters made showing reproductions of works of art, in order to draw the attention of the public to important artistic events at the *Louvre,* the *Orangerie* and the *Petit Palais.* Painters were the first to recognize the possibilities of this venture, and they became eager to try their hand at the new technique.

8

One of the first was Raoul Dufy, who agreed to paint a composition to announce an exhibition of French art in the Scandinavian countries. Later, in 1946, Picasso designed the poster for an exhibition held in Vallauris, by his potter friends.

Thus the start was given to a fashion that is by way of becoming a tradition; and if the present abundance should bring to light a few first-class works, we can but rejoice.

In this first volume, I have preferred to present only seven artists, all of whom are among the most important in contemporary painting. (The posters of Lautrec and Bonnard have already been discussed elsewhere*; other, important, artists have never turned their attention to the problem.)

In the catalogue that follows the reproductions, it will be noticed that several of our painters who, because they had been frequent visitors to printing plants were familiar with the technique, have themselves, unaided, engraved their posters. I might add that I, personally, have had the honor of welcoming to my shop on the Rue de Chabrol, practically all of the greatest contemporary artists, as well as certain younger men who are interested in the graphic arts.

Finally, it should be pointed out that reproductions of works chosen by the artists from their own *œuvre,* to serve as subjects for illustrating their exhibition posters, and frequently with remarkable results, cannot, however, be considered as originals.

Although handicapped by their sensitivity, in a branch of art that has little use for discretion, painters did not fear com-

---

* *Les Affiches de Toulouse-Lautrec,* by E. Jullien (Sauret éditeur). *Bonnard lithographe,* by Claude Roger-Marx (Sauret éditeur).

parison of their works with those of specialized poster makers. It is a fact, too, that every time they have used the means inherent to their own art, bringing into play suitability and distinction of color combinations, as also balance of forms, and without striving especially for showiness, they have produced harmonious works which, despite their reduced surface, have successfully withstood the test of street display. It may also be said that some of their placards, produced with the care demanded by the importance they attached to them, are real works of art. To obtain the results they wanted, I have seen Matisse, Picasso, or Chagall, tear up their original sketch and make a new one, printing of which they supervised with the most vigilant attention.

Thus, the present work should be of interest not only to the curious, who like to know what goes on off-stage, but also to all who take pleasure in what is called *la petite histoire* or, shall we say, the anecdotal foot-notes, to the history of art.

Readers are reminded that certain of these posters which did not attract especial attention at the time they appeared, have remained little known. One can only regret, for the peace of mind of collectors, that they should also have become extremely rare.

RAOUL DUFY composed few posters himself. This great artist, who was a keen investigator of all branches of artistic activity — he had great taste as a decorator and was a remarkable draftsman — was entirely familiar with printing techniques and would have made some excellent posters had he been interested to continue working in that branch.

His illustrations for Alphonse Daudet's *Tartarin de Taras-*

con belong among the masterpieces of color lithography. And his four original posters reproduced in the present volume, make us regret that such an indefatiguable artist as he was did not have the time to produce other works in this field. We may be sure that he would have applied the same skill and conscientiousness to these creations that he brought to everything he undertook.

Being unable to devote himself to this task, he had to be satisfied with choosing from among his paintings, or his water-colors, those to be reproduced as posters for his exhibitions. He nevertheless followed the different stages of their production very closely.

The work of FERNAND LÉGER had a profound influence both on the graphic arts and on decoration.

He was a born poster-maker who possessed all the necessary gifts of synthesis, force and brilliance, and it is to be wondered at that the walls of Paris should not be covered with his posters; doubtless no important firm approached him — discretion being the better part of valor — or perhaps he himself refused.

Léger was a regular visitor to our printing establishment, where he made a great number of lithographs in the form of prints and illustrations. He was also always happy to compose a poster. 'Well, Fernando, as he used to call me, how do you like this one? You know I must have good colors...'

This warm friend left only regrets behind him, and his memory remains alive in each one of us. In addition to his talent, we had the greatest esteem for his simplicity and friendliness.

I first met HENRI MATISSE in 1937, at the time of the *Exposition des Maîtres de l'Art Indépendant,* held in the *Petit Palais.*

We had printed the reproduction of one of his canvases, *Le Rêve,* chosen by him. Color proofs of the poster had been submitted to him in his studio which, at that time, was on the Boulevard Montparnasse. After making several superimpositions, he had asked us to return his canvas and, putting it aside, transformed the reproduction to suit his taste, at the same time correcting the text.

Henri Matisse had a lively interest in engraved texts and fine printing. Indeed, he personally chose the type for nearly all his books, and himself organized the title lay-outs as well as the blanks and spaces on the printed pages.

The subject of the second poster of the *Exposition des Maîtres de l'Art Indépendant* was *Le Petit Déjeuner,* by Bonnard, with whom I was also in contact in connection with the printing. This great artist gave me very explicit directions for reproducing his painting. Looking back on it, I think that Raymond Escholier who, at that time, was Curator of the *Petit Palais,* was to be congratulated on his choice of men to be the standard bearers of his exhibition.

Since then, I have frequently had the privilege of working with Henri Matisse, both after he retired to work in Nice, and on his visits to Paris. His original sketch of the poster was made to correspond to the size of the reproduction, and there was never any question of little tricks or printing a color which was not exactly the right shade. I recall one typical example of the attention that Henri Matisse gave to each detail of these productions.

While the poster for *Jazz* was being made, the date of the opening was set forward, and I had only a few days in which to finish it. I was therefore unable to submit the printed texts to the artist, and Bérès, the publisher, asked me to choose the type, which I did, with fairly good results. A few days later, I received a long letter from Henri Matisse, which, although friendly, was also rather severe. He criticized my choice and, needless to say, all the right was on his side.

If, here and there, people are kind enough to praise the printing done by my firm, is it not due to the fact that I have had this excellent schooling? Indeed, I should have been more than heedless not to have benefited from the lessons of such masters as these.

Thank you, therefore, dear Monsieur Matisse. I can say here that I recall all these great artists, now gone, with genuine emotion and gratitude.

The years during which GEORGES BRAQUE came most frequently to the print-shop were those between 1942 and 1945. At that time, there were no automobiles, and I can still see him arriving in the Rue de Chabrol on an incredible bicycle that was a cross between an old tricycle and a bulldozer. If he should chance to read these lines, our good friend will smile to hear that his arrival was awaited not only with pleasure — that goes without saying — but also for the spectacle it offered. There was no question of posters then. However, he was working on some lithographs, and the change of scene (it's a long way from the Parc Montsouris to the Gare de l'Est), the rather extraordinary setup of the old printing establishment, association with the printers — all of that Georges Braque liked, and he never hesitated to come all the way across Paris to make a few slight alterations.

Since that time, Braque has produced his lithographs mainly on transfer paper. Proofs are submitted to him, but frequently it is only after he has made numerous corrections that we obtain his final approval. The problem of the poster has also interested him very much and, several times, after making a highly perfect original, he has himself made the transfer to stone.

Since his return from America, in 1950, it is rare that MARC CHAGALL has not visited the print-shop each time he came to Paris. Indeed a vast amount of important work in progress has made it necessary for him to do so. But he also feels at home there. He enjoys the 'Beggars' Opera' atmosphere, and is welcomed by everybody with the greatest affection.

After having drawn in the principal color of his poster, Chagall has often permitted himself to make corrections and actually finish his sketch on the secondary color stones. How is it possible to resist the temptation to intensify a shade, or change a detail, when you have only to go down one flight to have access to the machine that is printing your work?

Thus, close collaboration is established between artists and artisans, and it is doubtless as a result of this team spirit, which machinery, thank heavens, has not yet replaced, that we obtain a quality of workmanship which, however imperfect, is nevertheless entirely individual, in other words, human.

Conceived, brought forth, watched over and supervised by the artist himself, in an atmosphere of creative excitement, all these posters are original, living works, in the same degree that valuable prints, lithographs and etchings are.

Except for the very first one, which was printed for the *Salon des Surréalistes,* while he was in the United States, JOAN MIRÓ has produced all his posters either on stone or on zinc. His poetic instinct inspires his choice of unforeseen elements which he succeeds in incorporating in his lithographs, thanks to long experience of the medium. Miró has always worked in the same shop, with the same men handling the presses. He draws in the different colors of his composition slowly and carefully, with the concentration and conscientiousness that he brings to everything he does. The result, always unexpected, is a veritable fireworks of color.

Beginning in october 1946, PICASSO came to work at the Rue de Chabrol during a period of several months. Every day, like any ordinary lithographic designer, he would arrive at nine o'clock, and until eight in the evening, sometimes later, he stayed there bent over his stones. Usually it was one of our men who waited for him and, because of the hour, had to ask him to stop. In reality, this was rather extra-ordinary for, as everyone knows, Pablo, like all the Spanish, is a late riser. But he liked doing this work, and having told none of his friends where he was going, he could apply him-self to it undisturbed. His friend, Jaime Sabartés, has given an excellent account of these few months spent working in a medium which was new to him*. During this period, Picasso exhausted the possibilities of the process; he both learned and re-invented lithography. It was therefore a simple matter for him when he approached poster-making.

* *Picasso lithographe,* volume I (Sauret éditeur).

After he retired to the south of France, he continued making lithographs on the zinc, stones and papers that I sent him. But the atmosphere of the workshop, with its blue-overalled printers and the noise of the machines, was lacking.

Since then, Picasso has been making engravings on lino-leum, and his posters for pottery shows and bullfights are printed by the type-setters in Vallauris, under the direction of Arnera. He himself, of course, continues to supervise the printing, and I know that my friend and colleague Arnera often has to wash his machine and start applying his color all over again, because it is not exactly the desired shade.

But artistic lithography is not limited to these brilliant champions. Famous young painters, others more painters than famous, some less young, some figurative and others non-figurative, are sufficiently attracted by the print-shop to enjoy working there, and their lithographic work will un-doubtedly furnish material for further study.

Meanwhile, if at times I have seemed to overestimate the *rôle* of the printer, we hope that the reader will not see in this a sinful pride, but on the contrary, a desire to do justice to the artisans — designers and others — who collaborate with the artist, who both share his apprehensions and rejoice at the success that crowns their diligence and his talent. This joy that derives from work well done, is the earthly reward most prized by men of good will.

F. M.

GEORGES BRAQUE

GALERIE MAEGHT
13 RUE DE TEHERAN 8ᵉ LAB. 16-43

G. BRAQUE

GALERIE MAEGHT
13 RUE DE TEHERAN 8ᵉ LAB. 16-43

ŒUVRE
GRAPHIQUE
DE
G. BRAQUE

GALERIE MAEGHT

G Braque

4

GALERIE MAEGHT

THEOGONIE

G. BRAQUE

8

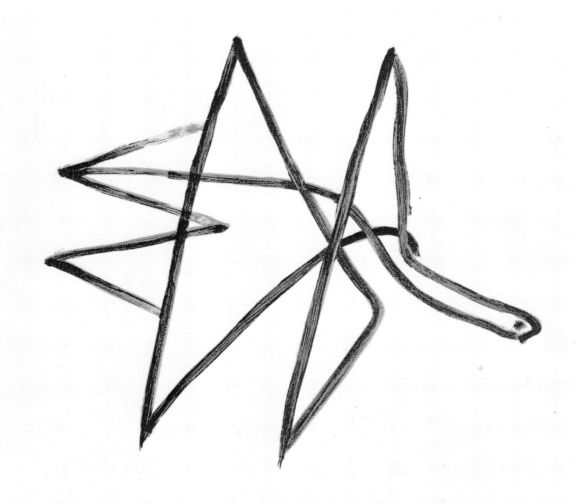

SPONSORED BY THE EDINBURGH FESTIVAL SOCIETY
AND ARRANGED BY THE ARTS COUNCIL OF GREAT BRITAIN IN ASSOCIATION WITH THE ROYAL SCOTTISH ACADEMY

EDINBURGH FESTIVAL 1956   18 AUGUST · 15 SEPTEMBER
ROYAL SCOTTISH ACADEMY

WEEKDAYS 10-9 · SUNDAYS 2-5   ADMISSION 2D

GALERIE MAEGHT

SUR 4 MURS

ŒUVRE GRAPHIQUE

CABINET DES ESTAMPES
ESTAMPES
GALERIE NICOLAS RAUCH S.A.
LIVRES ILLUSTRES
5 PROMENADE DU PIN **GENÈVE** 2 PLACE DU PORT
DU II SEPTEMBRE AU 12 OCTOBRE 1958

MOURLOT

GALERIE ADRIEN MAEGHT

42 RUE DU BAC

MOURLOT · PARIS · OCTOBRE · 1958

MARC CHAGALL

Kunsthalle Basel

Chagall

4. Nov. bis 3. Dez. 1933

Täglich 10-12½, 2-5

Eintritt Fr. 1.10 Mitglieder frei

Sonntag 2-5

Mittwoch 5-7 | 55 Cts

Zeichnung Marc Chagall Typo: Jan Tschichold Benno Schwabe & Co., Basel

KUNSTHAUS ZÜRICH

CHAGALL

DEZEMBER 1950 - JANUAR 1951

VENCE
Cité des Fleurs et des Arts
FÊTES DE PAQUES
1953

L'original du dessin ci-dessus, offert par le maître **Marc CHAGALL**, sera vendu le lundi, aux enchères à l'américaine.

LE LIVRE ITALIEN
CONTEMPORAIN

GALERIE DES PONCHETTES : 77, Quai des Etats-Unis - NICE

Du 4 au 18 JUIN 1953

Tous les Jours de 10 h. à 12 heures et de 15 h. à 19 heures

VENCE

CITÉ DES ARTS ET DES FLEURS

FÊTES DE PÂQUES
1954

BIBLE
Marc Chagall
VERVE
33-34

ÉDITIONS VERVE - PARIS

MOURLOT · PARIS

CHAGALL

27. Oktober – 29. November   Kunsthalle   Bern

VILLE DE NICE

Marc Chagall

ŒUVRE GRAVÉ

GALERIE DES PONCHETTES

77 QUAI DES ÉTATS-UNIS - 1ᵉʳ FÉVRIER - 16 MARS 1958 - TOUS LES JOURS DE 10 A 18 H

RAOUL DUFY

TRAGÉDIE, COMÉDIE

1946
1956

Compagnie
Madeleine Renaud
Jean-Louis Barrault

MOURLOT PARIS

FERNAND LEGER

FERNAND LÉGER

EXPOSITION RÉTROSPECTIVE 1905 · 1946

MUSÉE NATIONAL D'ART MODERNE
AVENUE DU PRÉSIDENT WILSON

6 OCTOBRE · 13 NOVEMBRE 1949
TOUS LES JOURS DE 10 A 17 HEURES · SAUF LE MARDI

ÉDITIONS DES MUSÉES NATIONAUX · MOURLOT, PARIS

A PARTIR DU 2 JUIN 1951

FERNAND LÉGER

LES CONSTRUCTEURS

et Sculptures Polychromes.

MAISON DE LA PENSÉE FRANÇAISE
2 RUE DE L'ÉLYSÉE _ PARIS _VIII.

MOURLOT · PARIS

F. LÉGER

LOUIS CARRÉ · 10 AVENUE DE MESSINE · JUIN 1953

MOURLOT PARIS

F. LÉGER

Museum Morsbroich . Leverkusen
Februar 1955

MOURLOT . PARIS

FERNAND LÉGER

MUSÉE DE LYON
28 JUIN - 30 SEPTEMBRE 1955
OUVERT TOUS LES JOURS

FESTIVAL LYON-CHARBONNIÈRES
SYNDICAT D'INITIATIVE DE LYON

MOURLOT-PARIS

F. LÉGER

OEUVRES RÉCENTES

MAISON DE
LA PENSÉE FRANÇAISE

2, RUE DE L'ÉLYSÉE - PARIS VIII - 1954

A PARTIR DU 10 NOVEMBRE

MOURLOT PARIS

HENRI MATISSE

HENRI MATISSE

GALERIE MAEGHT - PARIS

HENRI MATISSE

JAZZ

TERIADE EDITEUR

EXPOSITION

CHEZ

PIERRE BERÈS

14, AVENUE DE FRIEDLAND . PARIS VIII

DU 3 AU 20 DÉCEMBRE 1947

MOURLOT - PARIS

Nice travail & Joie H. Matisse

EDITE PAR LE SYNDICAT D'INITIATIVE DE NICE
ET L'UNION MÉDITERRANÉENNE POUR L'ART MODERNE
MOURLOT IMP. PARIS

HENRI MATISSE

ŒUVRES RÉCENTES
1947 - 1948

MUSÉE NATIONAL D'ART MODERNE
AVENUE DU PRÉSIDENT WILSON

DU 17 JUIN AU 25 SEPTEMBRE 1949

TOUS LES JOURS, SAUF LE MARDI, DE 10 HEURES A 17 HEURES

ÉDITIONS DES MUSÉES NATIONAUX - MOURLOT.PARIS

Madame de Pompadour
reçoit le mardi 20 novembre 1951
au Pavillon de Marsan
à 22 heures

H. MATISSE 51

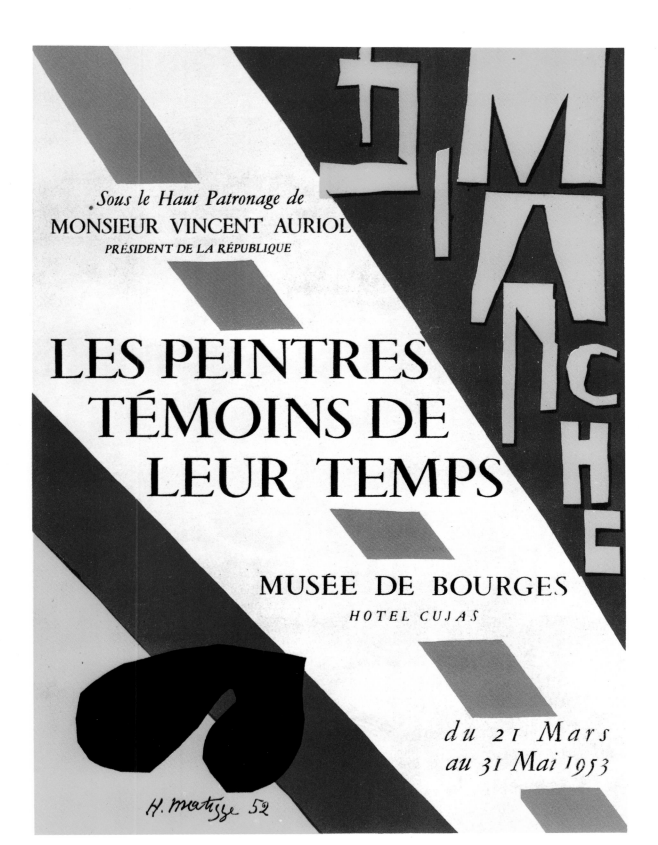

Sous le Haut Patronage de
MONSIEUR VINCENT AURIOL
PRÉSIDENT DE LA RÉPUBLIQUE

LES PEINTRES
TÉMOINS DE
LEUR TEMPS

MUSÉE DE BOURGES
HOTEL CUJAS

du 21 Mars
au 31 Mai 1953

H. Matisse 52

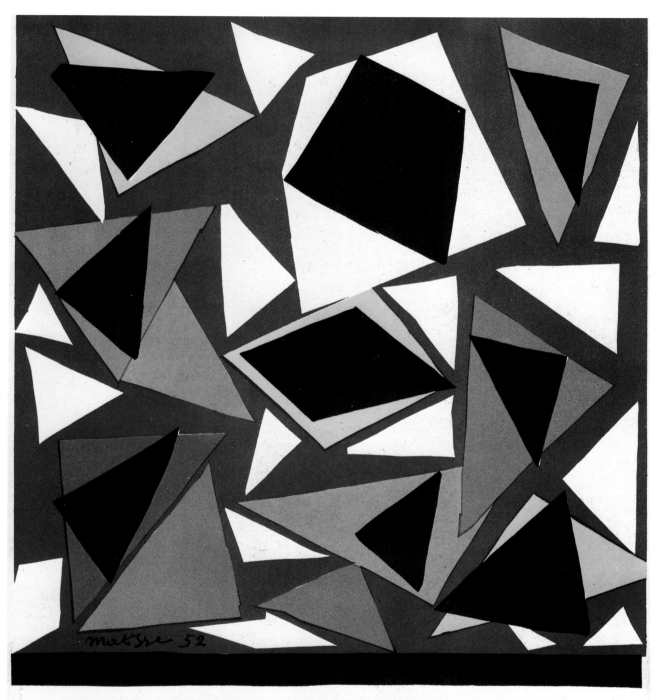

AFFICHES D'EXPOSITIONS RÉALISÉES DEPUIS 25 ANS
PAR L'IMPRIMERIE MOURLOT ET PRÉSENTÉES A L'OCCASION
DE SON CENTENAIRE A LA GALERIE KLÉBER, PARIS
24, AVENUE KLÉBER - 5 DÉCEMBRE 1952 - JANVIER 1953

THE ARTS COUNCIL
THE SCULPTURE OF MATISSE
AND THREE PAINTINGS WITH STUDIES

9 JANUARY - 22 FEBRUARY 1953
THE TATE GALLERY
WEEKDAYS 10-6   SUNDAYS 2-6   ADMISSION 1./-

H. Matisse.

MOURLOT PARIS

46

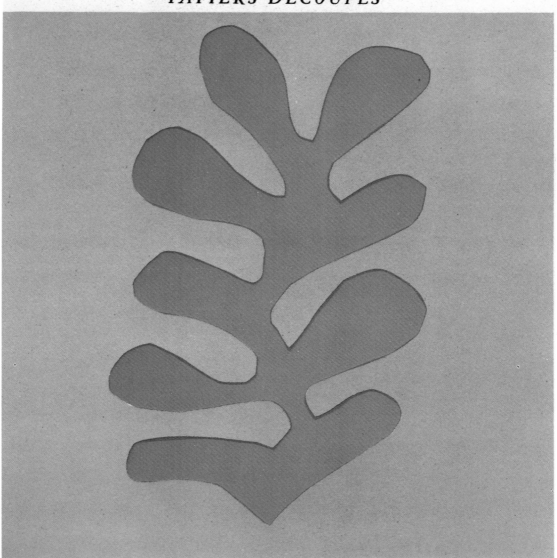

JOAN MIRÓ

E XPOSITION
INTERNATIONALE DU
SURRÉALISME
1 9 4 7
GALERIE MAEGHT
13 RUE DE TÉHÉRAN PARIS

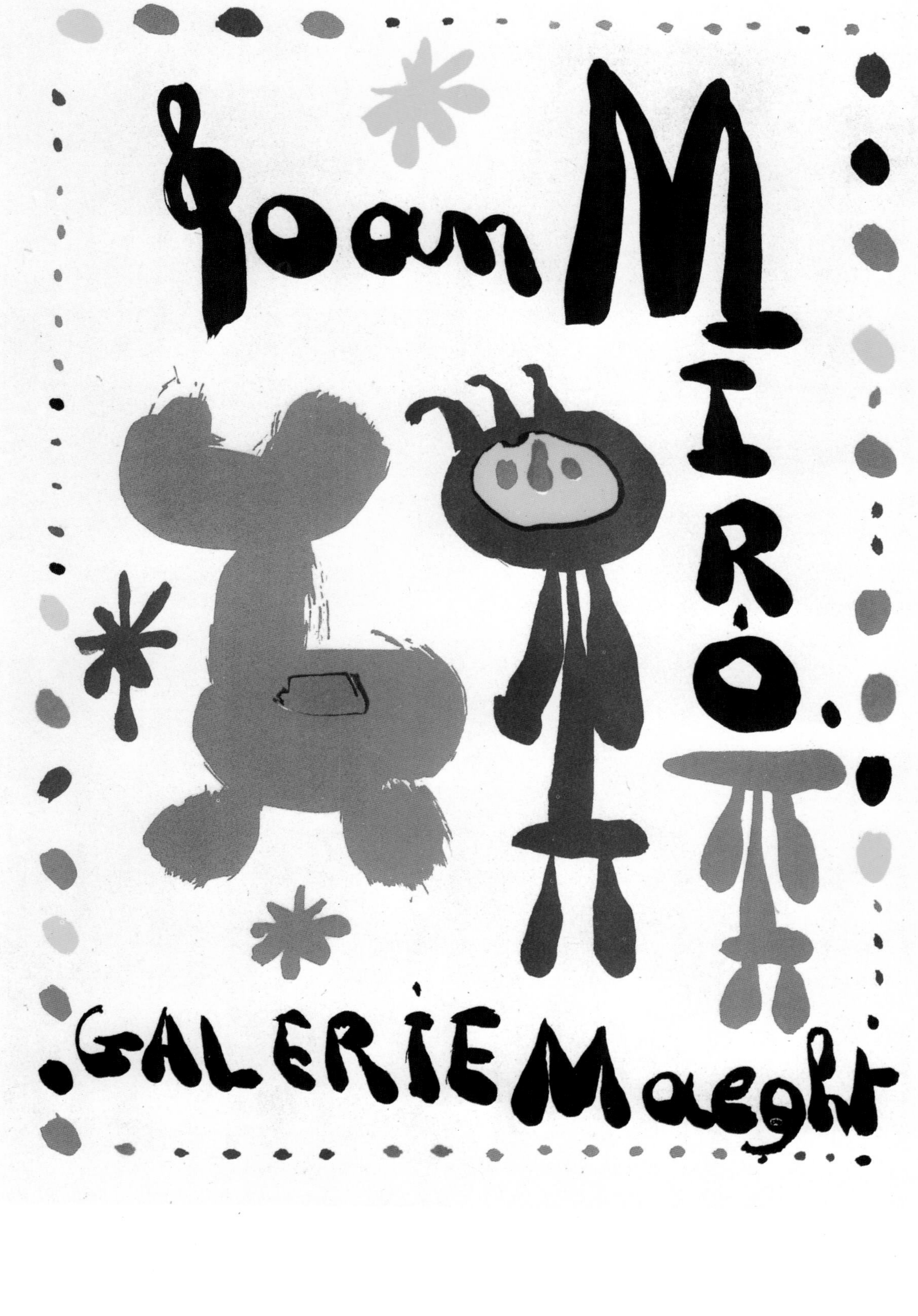
Joan Miró.
GALERIE Maeght

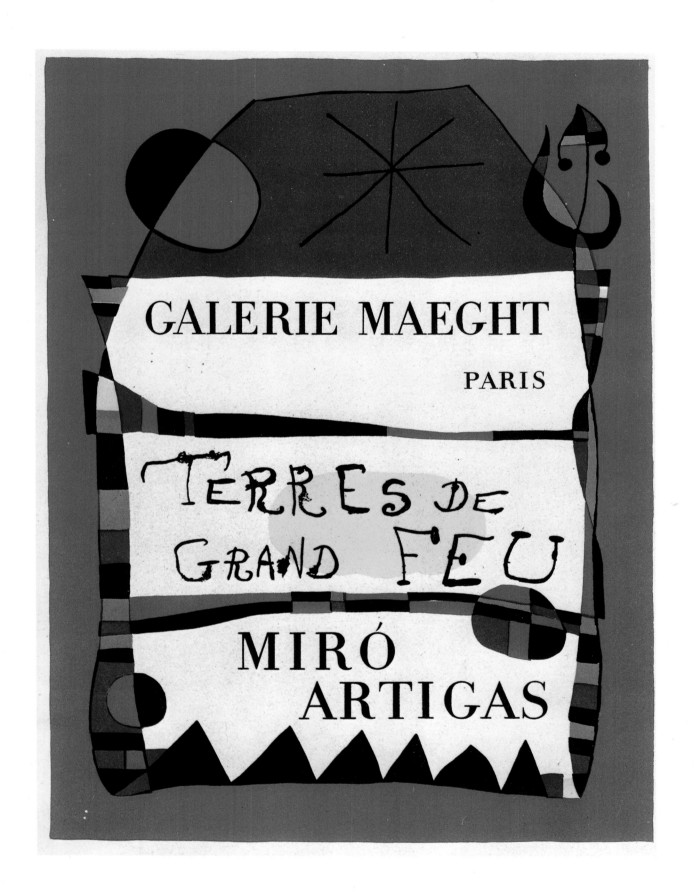

PEINTURES   *Miro*   SCULPTURES

LITHOGRAPHIES   CÉRAMIQUES

GALERIE MATARASSO 36 Bᵈ DUBOUCHAGE NICE

DU 17 MAI AU 17 JUIN 1957

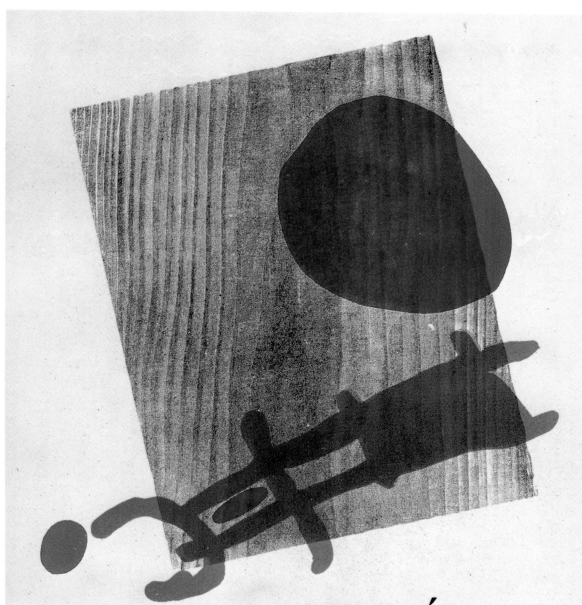

JOAN MIRÓ

bois gravés pour

A TOUTE ÉPREUVE de PAUL ELUARD

GÉRALD CRAMER ÉDITEUR

EXPOSITION CHEZ

BERGGRUEN & CIE

du 25 avril au 17 mai 1958   70, rue de l'Université Paris-VII

IMP. FEQUET ET BAUDIER, PARIS

PABLO PICASSO

EXPOSITION

DU 24 JUILLET AU 29 AOUT

POTERIES
FLEURS
PARFUMS
VALLAURIS
.A.M.

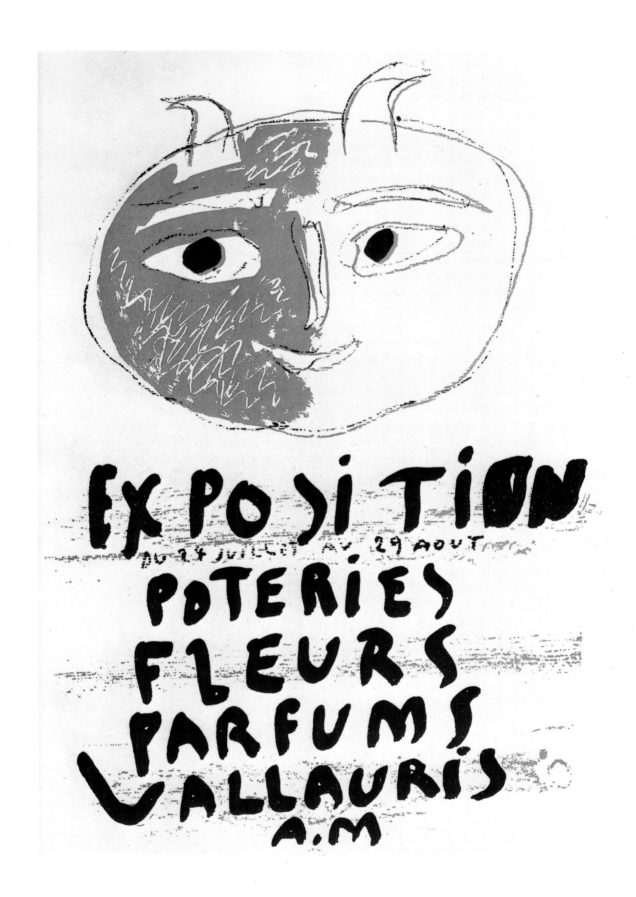

POTERIES
DE
PICASSO

DU 27 NOVEMBRE 1948
AU 5 JANVIER 1949

à la Maison de la Pensée Française

2, RUE DE L'ÉLYSÉE · PARIS

TOUS LES JOURS DE 10 HEURES A MIDI ET DE 14 A 19 HEURES

MOURLOT, IMP. PARIS

CONGRÈS MONDIAL
DES PARTISANS
DE LA PAIX

SALLE PLEYEL
20·21·22 ET 23 AVRIL 1949
PARIS

RELAIS DE LA JEUNESSE
DU 31 JUILLET AU 15 AOUT 1950
SOUS LE PATRONAGE DE LA REVUE "LES PARTISANS DE LA PAIX"

RENCONTRE INTERNATIONALE DE NICE
DU 13 AU 20 AOUT 1950
POUR L'INTERDICTION ABSOLUE DE L'ARME ATOMIQUE

VOS PLUS BELLES VACANCES
AIDERONT A SAUVER
LA PAIX

RENSEIGNEMENTS ET ADHÉSIONS
AU COMITÉ D'INITIATIVE NATIONAL · 19, RUE SAINT-GEORGES · PARIS 9e

MOURLOT IMP. PARIS

DEUXIÈME
CONGRÈS
MONDIAL
DES PARTISANS
DE LA PAIX
LONDRES
13-19 NOVEMBRE 1950

MOURLOT IMP. PARIS

EXPOSITION HISPANO-AMERICAINE

GALERIE
HENRI TRONCHE
6 AV PERCIER

30 NOVEMBRE
22 DECEMBRE
1951
PARIS

EXPOSITION HISPANO-AMERICAINE

GALERIE
HENRI TRONCHE
6 AU PERCIER

20 NOVEMBRE
22 DECEMBRE
1951
PARIS

CONGRÈS
DES PEUPLES
POUR LA PAIX

VIENNE
12-18 DÉCEMBRE 1952

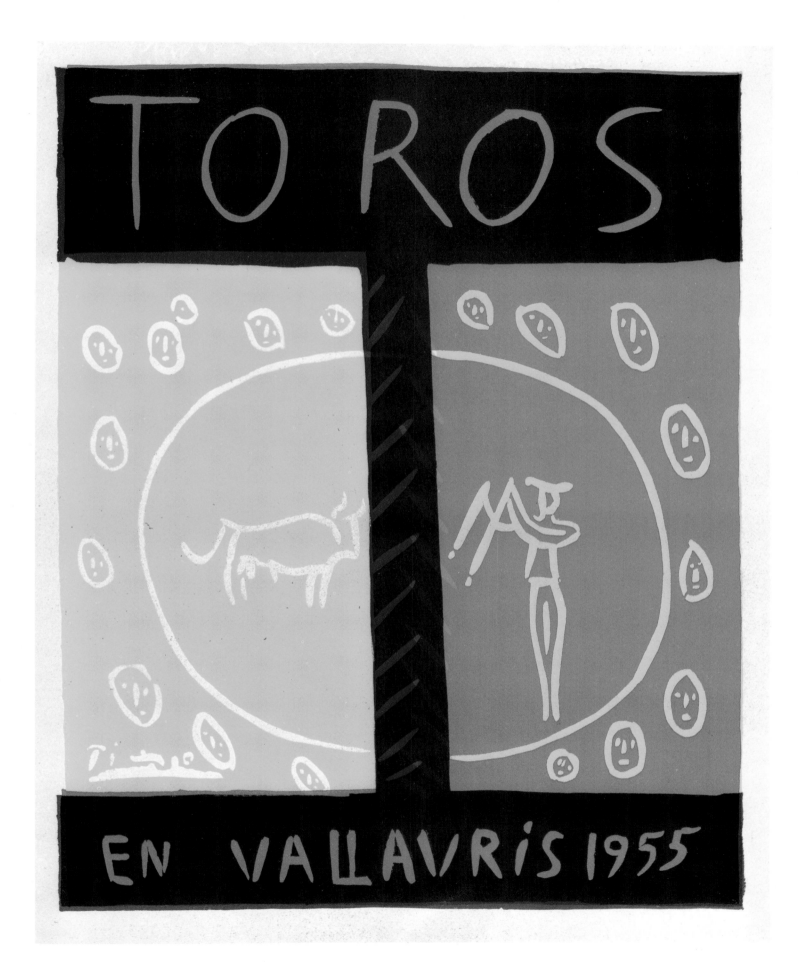

Hommage des
artistes Espagnols
au poète Antonio
Machado

Exposition

peinture – Sculpture
du 4 au 24 Février 1955

Maison de la Pensée Française
2 Rue de l'Elysée
PARiS VIII

Picasso
le 3.1.55.

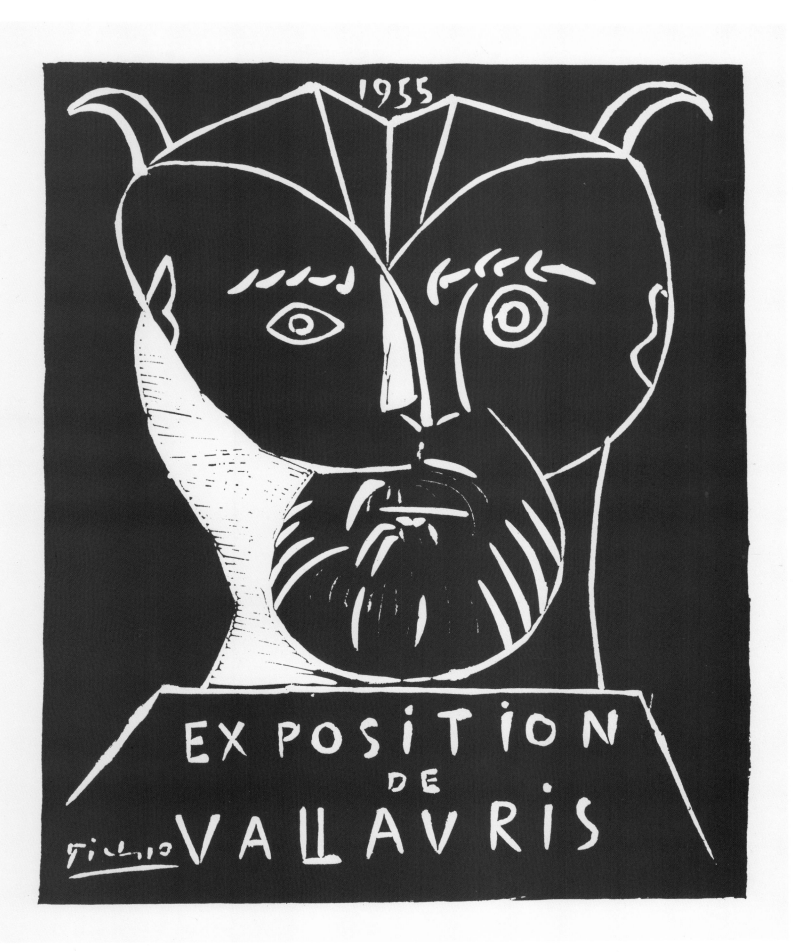

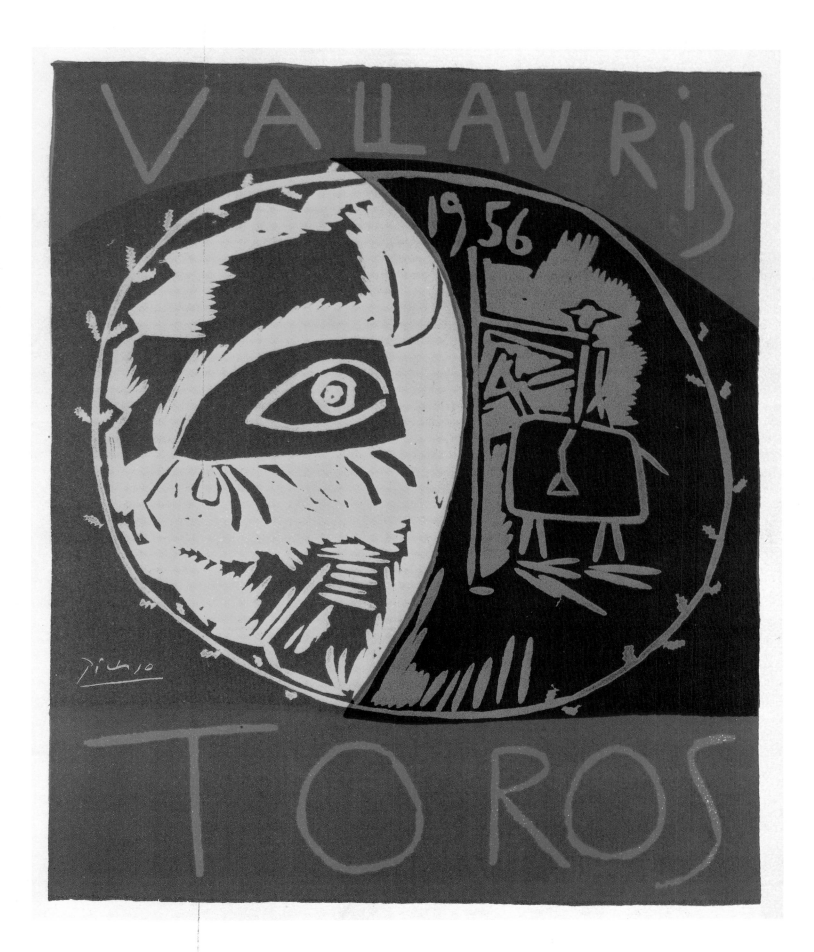

EXPOSITION
Peinture

VALAURIS
1956

PICASSO
Un demi-siècle de Livres Illustrés

du 21 Décembre 1956 au 31 Janvier 1957

GALERIE H. MATARASSO
36 Boulevard Dubouchage . NICE

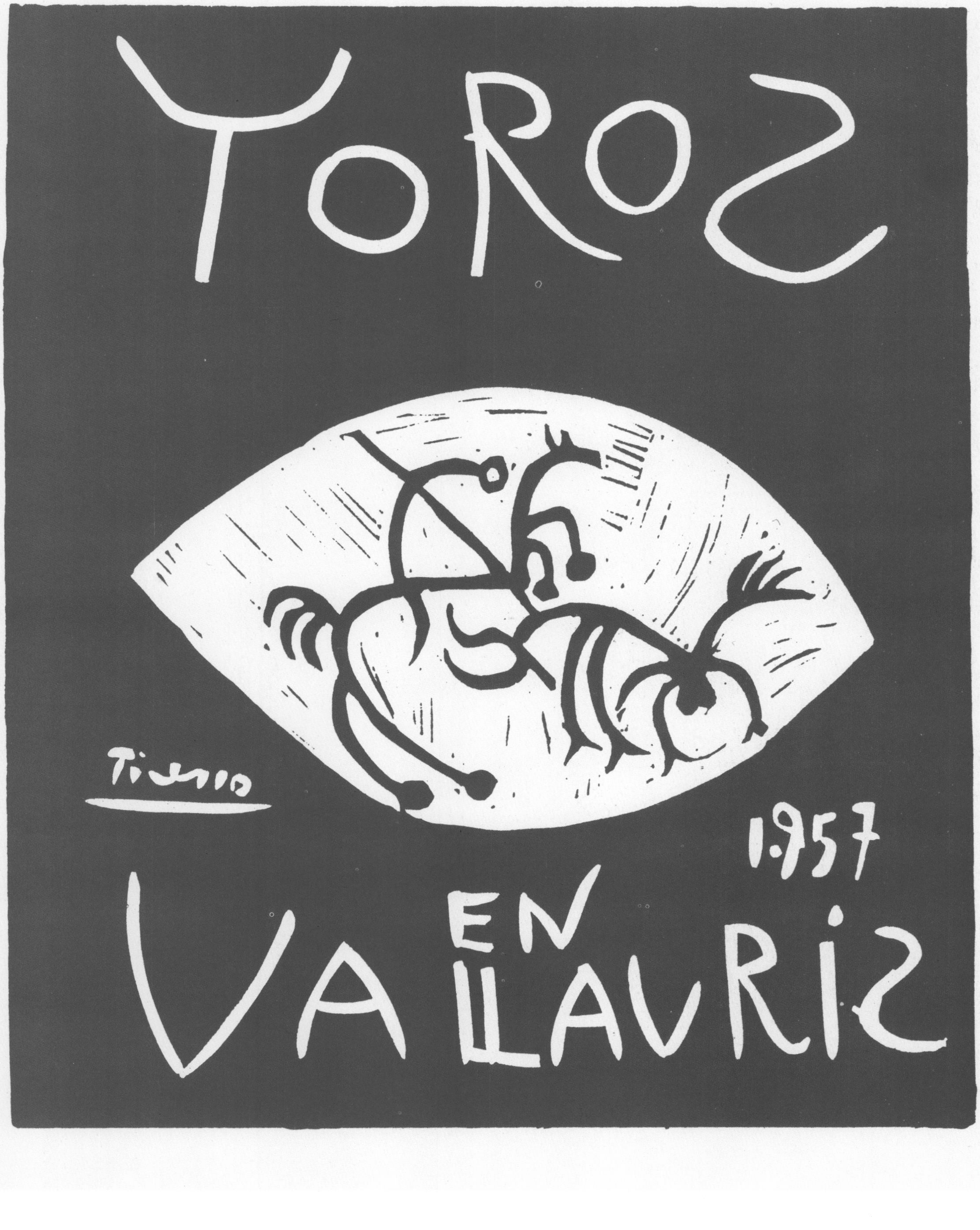
TOROS
1.957
EN
VALLAURIS

PiCASSO
PEINTURES
1955—1956
GALERIE LOUISE LEIRIS
47 Rue de Monceau—PARIS—VIII
mars—avril 1957.

GALERIE 65 - Cannes
65 R. d'Antibes - T. 915-33

Picasso

PATES BLANCHES
Empreintes originales Editées par Madoura
ET
Gravures Rares
EXPOSITION du 9 Août au 31 Août 1957

MUSÉE D'ART MODERNE
CÉRET
AOUT · SEPTEMBRE · OCTOBRE 1957

MOURLOT. IMP.

PATES BLANCHES

(Empreintes originales Madoura)

Picasso

GALERIE FOLKLORE

2 R. de Jussieu — Lyon
du 7.12 au 4.1.58.

IMP ARNERA - VALLAURIS

Maison de la Pensée Française,
2 Rue de l'Elysée

Exposition de Céramiques
du 8 mars au 30 juin
PICASSO

Picasso
6 14·1·58.

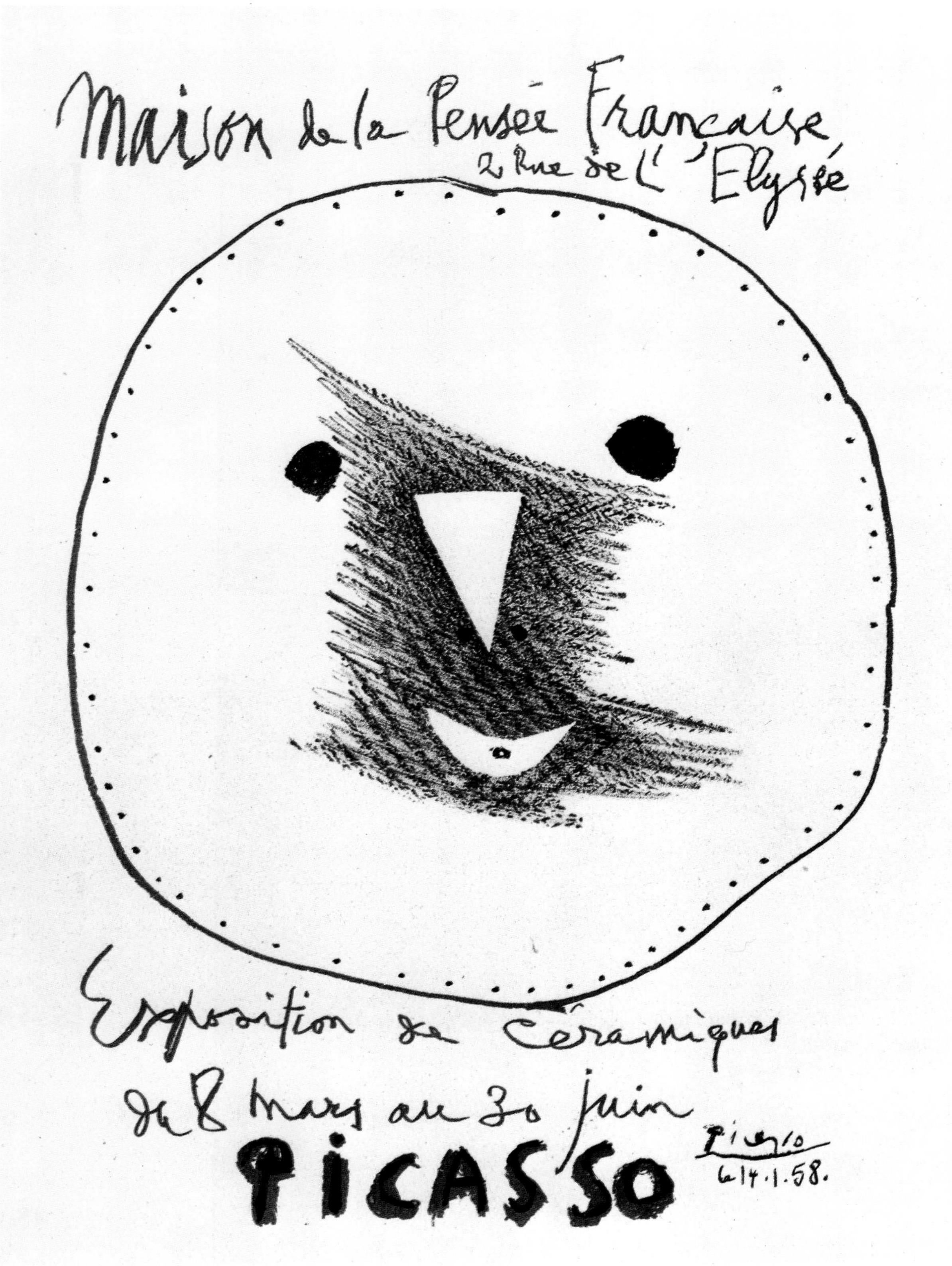
Maison de la Pensée Française,
2 Rue de l'Elysée
Exposition de Céramiques
du 8 mars au 30 juin
PICASSO

VALLAVRIS

dix ans de céramique
de
PiCASSO
plus
100 potiers - oevres
récentes

Hall Nézolium ————
19 juillet — 28 septembre

*The five posters
numbered 98 to 102 were made by Braque,
Chagall, Miró and Picasso during the summer
of 1959, while the present volume was in the
press. The editors have felt that their inclusion
could only enhance the interest of the collection.*

HOMMAGE A SA MÉMOIRE

COLLIOURE, 22 FÉVRIER 1959

PARIS, 25 FÉVRIER

ANNEXE DE LA SORBONNE

GALERIE MAEGHT

Marc Chagall

MUSÉE DES ARTS DÉCORATIFS - PALAIS DU LOUVRE

PAVILLON DE MARSAN, 107 RUE DE RIVOLI _ TOUS LES JOURS DE 10 H. A 17 H. SAUF LE MARDI

JOAN MIRO
Constellations
PIERRE MATISSE ÉDITEUR
EXPOSITION CHEZ
BERGGRUEN - 70 RUE DE L'UNIVERSITÉ - PARIS
MOURLOT IMP. PARIS

PICASSO

"Les Ménines"
Galerie Louise Leiris
47. Rue de Monceau
du 22 mai au 27.6.59.

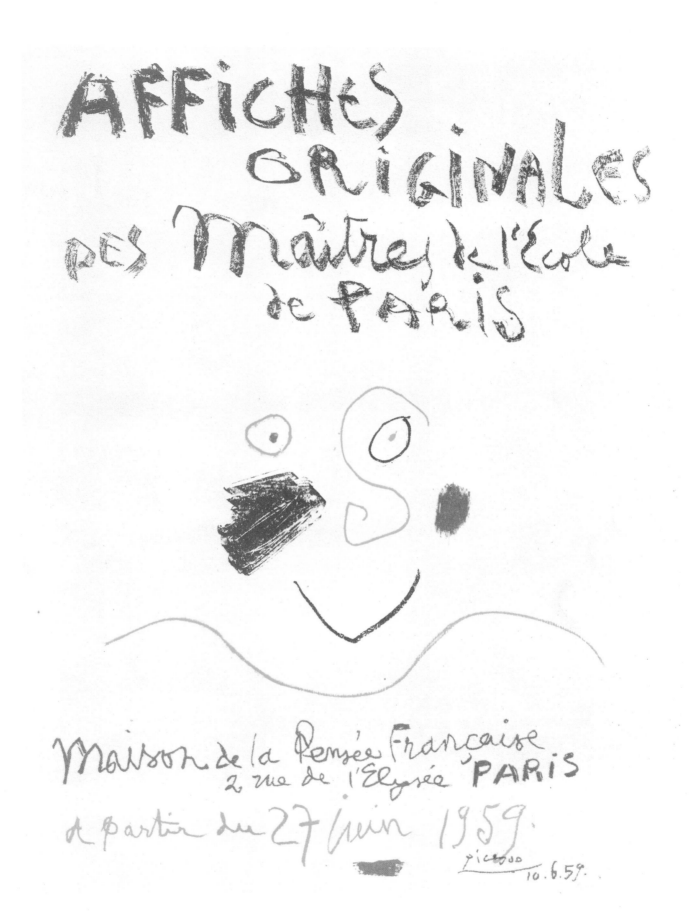

DESCRIPTIVE
CATALOGUE

GEORGES BRAQUE

1 G. BRAQUE.   Maeght Gallery, Paris. 1946.
   200 prints, 61 × 48 format, lithographic print in six colors, Mourlot Printers.
   The original sketch, in corresponding size, was made by mounting a drawing on a piece
   of corrugated cardboard.

2 ŒUVRE GRAPHIQUE.   Graphic works.   Maeght Gallery, Paris. 1947.
   300 prints, 59 × 44.5 format, lithographic print in four colors, Mourlot Printers.
   It was the artist's intention that this poster should recall the preceding one.

3 G. BRAQUE.   Maeght Gallery, Paris. 1950.
   275 prints, 73.5 × 52 format, lithographic print in seven colors, Mourlot Printers.

4 G. BRAQUE.   Maeght Gallery, Paris. 1952.
   250 prints, 62 × 48 format, lithographic print in seven colors, Mourlot Printers.
   50 prints on Arches paper.

5 THÉOGONIE.   Maeght Gallery, Paris. July 1954.
   250 prints, 75.5 × 55.5 format, lithographic print in five colors, Mourlot Printers.
   100 prints on Arches paper, before lettering.

6 SUR QUATRE MURS.   On four walls.   Maeght Gallery, Paris. 1956.
   250 prints, 72.5 × 42 format, lithographic print in eight colors, Mourlot Printers.
   100 prints on Arches paper, before lettering.

7 BRAQUE GRAVEUR.   Braque's engravings.
   Berggruen & Co. Gallery, Paris. November 1953.
   750 prints, 60.5 × 41.5 format, lithographic print in six colors, Mourlot Printers.
   The same subject was also used as the cover for the catalogue.
   Another, slightly enlarged, printing of this poster was made abroad, by offset.

8 G. BRAQUE.   Maeght Gallery, Paris. 1956.
   1,000 prints, 75 × 51.5 format, lithographic print in eight colors from an original sketch
   of corresponding size, made on newsprint, Mourlot Printers.
   100 prints on Arches paper.

9 G. BRAQUE EXHIBITION.   August 1958.
   350 prints for London, and 350 for the Royal Scottish Academy.
   73.5 × 52 format. Lithographic print in five colors, Mourlot Printers.

10 SUR QUATRE MURS.   On four walls.   Maeght Gallery, Paris. 1958.
    1,000 prints, 71.5 × 47.5 format, original lithograph in five colors, Mourlot Printers.
    75 proofs were made on Arches paper, before lettering, and signed by the artist.

11 ŒUVRE GRAPHIQUE.   Graphic works.   Nicolas Rauch, Geneva. September 1958.
    750 prints, 73.5 × 51 format, original lithograph in six colors, Mourlot Printers.
    75 prints made on Arches paper, before lettering, and signed by the artist.

12 ESTAMPES – LIVRES.   Engravings – Books.   Adrien Maeght, Paris. 1958.
    700 prints, 50 × 39.5 format, lithograph in three colors, Mourlot Printers.
    A few proofs on Arches paper were printed before lettering.

98 G. BRAQUE.   Maeght Gallery, Paris. June 1959.
    1,000 prints, 72 × 50 format, lithograph in six colors, Mourlot Printers.
    250 prints on Arches paper, before lettering.

MARC CHAGALL

13   CHAGALL.   Kunsthalle, Basel. November 1953.
      130 × 90 format, two colors, Benno Schwabe Printers, Basel.

14   CHAGALL.   Maeght Gallery, Paris. 1950.
      250 prints, 60 × 50 format, original lithograph in six colors, Mourlot Printers.
      50 prints on Arches paper, before lettering, and signed by the artist.

15   CHAGALL.   Kunsthaus, Zurich. December 1950.
      500 prints, 100 × 65 format, original lithograph in six colors, Mourlot Printers.
      50 prints on Arches paper, before lettering.

16   CHAGALL – CÉRAMIQUES – SCULPTURES.   Ceramics – Sculptures.   1952.
      250 prints, 69 × 54.5 format, original lithograph in eight colors, Mourlot Printers.
      200 prints on Arches paper, before lettering.

17   CHAGALL – PEINTURES – AQUARELLES – DESSINS.   Paintings – Watercolors –
      Drawings.
      Galerie des Ponchettes, Nice. February 1952.
      750 prints, 100 × 63 format, Mourlot Printers.
      A few prints on Arches paper, before lettering.
      Lithographic print in ten colors, from a gouache made by the artist in view of a poster
      for one of his exhibitions.   This poster was also used for an exhibition in Milan.

18   VENCE, FÊTES DE PÂQUES 1953.   Easter holidays 1953.   March 1953.
      104 × 69 format. — Imprimerie Meyerbeer, Nice.
      From a drawing made for this poster.

19   LE LIVRE ITALIEN CONTEMPORAIN.   Contemporary Italian books.
      Galerie des Ponchettes, Nice. June 1953.
      94 × 65 format. — Imprimerie Meyerbeer, Nice.
      From a drawing made for this poster.

20   VENCE, FÊTES DE PÂQUES 1954.   Easter holidays 1954.   March 1954.
      750 prints, 100 × 63 format, original lithograph in eight colors, Mourlot Printers.
      A few prints on Arches paper, before lettering.

21   PARIS.   Maeght Gallery, Paris. June 1954.
      750 prints, 71 × 47.5 format, lithographic reproduction in eleven colors, Mourlot Printers.
      200 proofs on Arches paper, before lettering, numbered and signed.

22   BIBLE.   *Verve,* Paris. October 1956.
      800 prints, 63 × 42 format, original lithograph in six colors, Mourlot Printers.
      50 proofs on Arches paper, before lettering, and signed by the artist.

23   MARC CHAGALL – GOUACHEN – AQUARELLE.   Gouaches – Watercolors.
      Salzburg, 1957.
      83 × 58 format, lithographic print in five colors.

24   CHAGALL.   Maeght Gallery, Paris. June 1957.
      1,000 prints, 66.5 × 45.5 format, original lithograph in four colors.
      50 proofs on Arches paper, before lettering, and signed by the artist.

25   CHAGALL.   Kunsthalle, Berne. October 1957.
      126.5 × 90 format. Original lithograph in five colors.

MARC CHAGALL   (Continued)

26   ŒUVRE GRAVÉ.   Graphic works.   Galerie des Ponchettes, Nice. February 1958.
      500 prints, 65 × 48 format, lithographic print in eight colors, Mourlot Printers.
      A few proofs on Arches paper, before lettering, but which bear the title CHAGALL.
      This is a reproduction by means of photolithography of an original lithograph by Chagall
      (Maeght Editions), reduced and designed for a poster.

99   CHAGALL.   Musée des Arts décoratifs, Paris. June 1959.
      1,500 prints, 75 × 51 format, original lithograph in four colors, Mourlot Printers.
      40 proofs on Arches paper, before lettering, and reserved for the artist.

RAOUL DUFY

27   SALON DES ARTISTES DÉCORATEURS.   Annual Decorators' Show.
      R. Bessard, Publisher. 1939.
      Lithograph in four colors, Karcher Printers, Paris.
      This poster was printed in two formats : 160 × 120 and 40 × 29.

28   EXPOSITION D'ART FRANÇAIS.   Kaunas (Lithuania). 1939.
      750 prints, 100 × 65 format, lithograph in six colors, Mourlot Printers.
      A few proofs were printed on Arches paper and given to the artist.
      Raoul Dufy designed this poster for an exhibition of contemporary French art that was to
      be held in Kaunas.   The posters were shipped and the text was to have been printed on
      the spot.   No one knows what became of the shipment.

29   PLANÉTARIUM.   1956.
      1,000 prints, 67 × 46 format, lithographic print in eight colors, Mourlot Printers.
      50 prints on Arches paper.

30   TRAGÉDIE – COMÉDIE.   1956.
      500 prints, 65 × 49 format, on thin Arches paper.
      Raoul Dufy had designed this poster for his friend Jean-Louis Barrault in 1954, in view
      of a theatrical tour in the United States.   It was not printed then, however, but in 1956,
      when this great actor had the poster published in tribute to his friend, Dufy.

FERNAND LÉGER

31   FERNAND LÉGER.   Musée national d'Art moderne, Paris. October 1949.
      500 prints, 73 × 52 format, lithograph in three colors, Mourlot Printers.

32   LES CONSTRUCTEURS.   The Builders.
      Maison de la Pensée française, Paris. June 1951.
      800 prints, 76 × 52 format, original lithograph in five colors, Mourlot Printers.

33   SCULPTURES POLYCHROMES.   Polychromatic sculptures.
      Louis Carré Gallery, Paris. January 1953.
      700 prints, 65.5 × 49 format, lithographic print in seven colors, Mourlot Printers.
      A few proofs on Arches paper.

34   LÉGER.   Louis Carré Gallery, Paris. June 1953.
      500 prints, 65.5 × 46.5 format, lithographic print in six colors, Mourlot Printers.
      100 prints on Arches paper.

FERNAND LÉGER   (Continued)

35 F. LÉGER.   Morsbroich Museum, February 1955.
500 prints, 76 × 56 format, lithograph in three colors, Mourlot Printers.
A few proofs before lettering, reserved for the artist.

36 FERNAND LÉGER.   Musée de Lyon, June 1955.
800 prints, 76.5 × 52 format, composition in four colors printed by means of lithography.
A few proofs before lettering, reserved for the artist.

37 ŒUVRES RÉCENTES.   Recent works.
Maison de la Pensée française, Paris. November 1954.
750 prints, 66 × 49 format, lithographic print in seven colors, Mourlot Printers.
With regard to this poster, Léger was particularly hard to please.   He came several
times to the print-shop and brought some last-moment corrections, after it was already
in press.   In the end, he was very satisfied, and the result is excellent.

HENRI MATISSE

38 EXPOSITION DE DESSINS.   Exhibition of drawings.   Maeght Gallery, Paris. 1945.
150 prints, 120 × 80 format.   In two colors.

39 JAZZ.   Pierre Berès Gallery, Paris. December 1947.
500 prints, 63 × 45.5 format, lithograph in two colors, Mourlot Printers.

40 TRAVAIL ET JOIE.   Work and joy.   City of Nice, 1948.
10,000 prints, 100 × 65 format, lithographic print in ten colors, Mourlot Printers.

41 ŒUVRES RÉCENTES.   Recent works.
Musée national d'Art moderne, Paris. 1949.
500 prints, 73 × 52 format, enlargement of an original linoleum-cut especially engraved
for this poster, Mourlot Printers.

42 HENRI MATISSE.   Maison de la Pensée francaise, Paris. July 1950.
700 prints, 76 × 53 format.   Paper cut-out, corresponding in size, printed lithographically, in four colors, Mourlot Printers.

43 BAL DE L'ÉCOLE DES ARTS DÉCORATIFS.   Annual ball of the School of Decorative Arts.
Pavillon de Marsan, Paris. November 20, 1951.
1,500 prints, 80 × 60 format, lithographic print in ten colors, Mourlot Printers.
A few proofs on Arches paper were reserved for the artist.   Matisse composed this
magnificent design with paper cut-outs on which he later drew with the brush.
The original was donated for the benefit of the alumni of the School of Decorative Arts.

44 LES PEINTRES TÉMOINS DE LEUR TEMPS.   Painters as witnesses of their time.
Paris and Bourges, 1952.
800 prints, 51.5 × 37.5 format, lithograph in four colors made from a collage, Mourlot
Printers.
Printed with two different texts : PARIS and BOURGES.

45 EXPOSITION D'AFFICHES.   Poster show.   Kléber Gallery, Paris. 1952.
800 prints, 65 × 50 format, French and Dutch text, Mourlot Printers.
A few proofs on Arches paper, before lettering, reserved for the artist.   Six-color lithograph made from a collage composed for a poster exhibition organized in honor of the
centennial of the Mourlot Brothers' printing house.   This composition is one of the early,
very successful examples of abstract art published for a wide public.

HENRI MATISSE   (Continued)

46 THE SCULPTURE OF MATISSE.
   The Tate Gallery, London. 1953.
   800 prints, 75.5 × 52.5 format.   A composition of collage and drawing, printed lithographically, in five colors, Mourlot Printers.

47 MATISSE, PAPIERS DÉCOUPÉS.   Paper cut-outs.
   Berggruen & Co. Gallery, Paris. 1953.
   Two editions of 500 prints, 65 × 40 format.   Lithograph printed in two colors from a paper cut-out.   The first 500 copies printed by Desjobert; the second by Mourlot.

JOAN MIRÓ

48 EXPOSITION DU SURRÉALISME.   Surrealist exhibition.
   Maeght Gallery, Paris. 1947.
   200 prints, 65 × 47 format, composition made for this poster and printed in five-color lithography, Mourlot Printers.

49 JOAN MIRÓ.   Maeght Gallery, Paris. 1949.
   300 prints, 65 × 50 format, original lithograph in five colors, Mourlot Printers.
   75 proofs on Rives B. F. K. paper of a second version of this composition, revised and signed by the artist.

50 MIRÓ – ART GRAPHIQUE.   Graphic art.   Maeght Gallery, Paris. 1950.
   350 prints, 64.5 × 50 format, original lithograph in five colors, Mourlot Printers.
   40 proofs on Arches paper, before lettering, and signed by the artist.

51 MIRÓ – ŒUVRES RÉCENTES.   Recent works.   Maeght Gallery, Paris. 1953.
   350 prints, 67.5 × 50.5 format, original lithograph in eight colors, Mourlot Printers.

52 DERRIÈRE LE MIROIR.   Behind the mirror.   Maeght, publisher, Paris. 1954.
   500 prints, 38 × 25 format, original lithograph in four colors, Mourlot Printers.

53 TERRES DE GRAND FEU.   Maeght Gallery, Paris. 1955.
   500 prints, 68 × 51 format, original lithograph in five colors, Mourlot Printers.

54 MIRÓ.   Matarasso Gallery, Nice. 1957.
   500 prints, 67 × 49 format, original lithograph in five colors, Mourlot Printers.
   75 prints on Arches paper, before lettering, and signed by the artist.

55 À TOUTE ÉPREUVE.   Never-failing.   Berggruen & Co. Gallery, Paris. 1958.
   500 prints, 51.5 × 38, format, Féquet and Beaudier Printers.
   100 prints on Rives paper, before lettering, and signed by the artist, Lacourière Printers.
   Poster composed by Miró with the original wood-cuts contained in the book À toute épreuve, by Paul Éluard (Gérard Cramer, Publisher).

100 CONSTELLATIONS.   Berggruen & Co. Gallery, Paris. 1959.
   900 prints, 68 × 49 format, original lithograph in seven colors, Mourlot Printers.
   75 proofs on Arches paper, and signed by the artist.
   Poster published for the exhibition of the book, Constellations (Pierre Matisse, Publisher).

PABLO PICASSO

The letter 'M', followed by a number, indicates the number of the lithograph concerning which precise details may be found in the volume entitled Picasso lithographe, *published by André Sauret.*

56
57
58 EXPOSITION POTERIES, FLEURS, PARFUMS. Pottery – Flowers – Perfumes.
Vallauris, July 1948.
Picasso presented a poster to the municipality of Vallauris; but he made three different lithographs.
350 prints, 60 × 40 format, of each poster on *vélin du Marais* paper. Composition in two colors done on lithographic paper in wash and pencil, Mourlot Printers.
50 proofs on Arches paper, signed by the artist, of each one of the three compositions (M. 118-119-120).

59 POTERIES DE PICASSO. Pottery by Picasso.
Maison de la Pensée française, Paris. November 1948.
750 prints, 61 × 40 format, lithographic print in two colors, Mourlot Printers.

60 CONGRÈS MONDIAL DES PARTISANS DE LA PAIX. World Congress of Peace Partisans. Paris, April 1949.
1,500 prints, 120 × 80 format, and 1,000 prints, 60 × 40 format, on poster paper, Mourlot Printers.
The subject of this famous poster is identical with that of an original lithograph by Picasso (M. 141) which was photographically printed and has subsequently been reproduced in millions of copies throughout the world.

61 RELAIS DE JEUNESSE. Youth rally.   Nice, August 1950.
1,000 prints, 120 × 80 format, and 500 prints, 76 × 56 format, Mourlot Printers.
Picasso made an original lithograph (M. 188) for this poster from which 50 prints were pulled.   The printing of the poster, in 120 × 80 format, was made from a transported version of this lithograph.

62 DEUXIÈME CONGRÈS DE LA PAIX. Second Peace Congress.
London, November 1950.
2,000 prints, 120 × 80 format, French and English text, Mourlot Printers.
Picasso made three lithographic designs on zinc.   This dove in flight was chosen; the zinc design was then transferred to stone and printed in lithograph on china paper.
50 prints were pulled from each of the three zinc designs (M. 191, 192, 193).

63 EXPOSITION HISPANO-AMÉRICAINE.
Henri Tronche Gallery, Paris. December 1951.
400 prints, 65 × 49.5 format, and 100 prints by hand-press on vellum, signed by the artist.   Original lithograph, Mourlot Printers.

64
65 EXPOSITION HISPANO-AMÉRICAINE.
December 1951. Original lithographs.
A few proofs reserved for the artist.
50 prints, 65 × 49.5 format, of the two subjects, without lettering. (M. 204-205-206-207-208).
Picasso made three fairly similar designs.   The one referred to under no. 63 was the one eventually chosen for the poster.

66 EXPOSITION VALLAURIS 1951.
400 prints in tawny on white, 65 × 50 format, and 400 prints in green on white, on vellum.   Original linoleum-cut, Arnera Printers, Vallauris.

PABLO PICASSO (Continued)

67 CONGRÈS DES PEUPLES POUR LA PAIX. Peoples' Peace Congress.
Vienna, December 1952.
1,000 prints, 120 × 80 format, lithograph in eight colors, Mourlot Printers.
This poster has a long history. This, the seventh, version was the one Picasso finally selected (M. 210 to 216).

68 EXPOSITION VALLAURIS 1952.
This poster has been printed twice :

for Vallauris, on the original linoleum-cut, 70 × 50 format, 450 prints in black on white poster paper, 350 prints in black on canary yellow paper, 500 prints in black on orange paper, 500 prints in green on canary yellow paper, and 100 proofs on fine quality canary paper, signed by the artist, Arnera Printers ;

for Paris, when this exhibition was presented at the *Maison de la Pensée française*, the same subject, photographically reduced (no. 68), was brought out in an edition of 1,000 prints on different colored Canson papers, in 64 × 45 format. Picasso designed the lettering for this second edition, Mourlot Printers.

69 EXPOSITION VALLAURIS 1953.
2,000 prints, 67 × 51.5 format, a drawing done in black printed on poster paper painted with colored bands, Arnera Printers.

70 EXPOSITION VALLAURIS 1954.
600 prints, 69 × 54 format, original linoleum-cuts in two colors, Arnera Printers.

71 TOROS EN VALLAURIS 1954. Bulls in Vallauris.
240 prints, 96 × 76 format, 100 of which are signed by the artist. Original linoleum-cut, Arnera Printers.

72 SUITE DE 180 DESSINS. Collection of 180 drawings.
The review *Verve*, Paris. October 1954.
1,000 prints, 61 × 40 format. Original composition by Picasso, paper cut-outs and collage of the texts. The poster is lithographically printed in seven colors, same format as the original, Mourlot Printers.

73 HOMMAGE AU POÈTE ANTONIO MACHADO. Tribute to the poet Antonio Machado.
Paris, February 1955.
700 prints, 65 × 50 format. Reproduction in offset of a drawing in two colors. Imprimerie du Lion, Paris.

74 TOROS EN VALLAURIS 1955. Bulls in Vallauris 1955.
200 prints, 75 × 59 format, and signed by the artist. Original linoleum-cut in three colors, Arnera Printers.

75 EXPOSITION DE VALLAURIS 1955.
600 prints, 66 × 54 format, original linoleum-cut, Arnera Printers.

76 EXPOSITION VALLAURIS 1955.
600 prints, 66 × 55 format, original linoleum-cut, Arnera Printers.

77 EXPOSITION 55 VALLAURIS.
600 prints, 67 × 53 format, original linoleum-cut, Arnera Printers.

PABLO PICASSO (Continued)

78 EXPOSITION PICASSO.   Gallery 65, Cannes.
    1,000 prints on vellum and 100 numbered and signed prints on Arches vellum, 65 × 50 format.   Original lithograph in six colors, Mourlot Printers.
    A few prints of an uncorrected first version of this lithograph were made.

79 TOROS – VALLAURIS – 1956.   Bulls in Vallauris 1956.
    175 prints, 65 × 54 format, and signed by the artist.   Original linoleum-cut in four colors, Arnera Printers.

80 EXPOSITION VALLAURIS 1956.
    175 prints, 65 × 54 format, on Arches paper, and signed by the artist.   Original lino-leum-cut in five colors.   A fine achievement which demonstrates once more to what extent Picasso uses each technique to advantage.   The artist supervised the printing of all of the colors and the printer, Arnera, produced a very handsome edition.

81 EXPOSITION DE PEINTURE VALLAURIS 1956.   Paintings, Vallauris 1956.
    1,000 prints, 66 × 50 format.   Typolithographic print in five colors, from a water color in the same format, Arnera Printers.
    Picasso colored some of these posters by hand, and they were sold for the benefit of the Exhibit.

82 PICASSO – UN DEMI-SIÈCLE DE LIVRES ILLUSTRÉS.   Fifty years of illustrated books.
    Nice, December 1956.
    1,000 prints, 65 × 50 format, on vellum, and 200 prints on different *de luxe* papers, signed by the artist.   Printing in three colors.
    Picasso drew a design on zinc with a lithographic pencil, printing of which was success-fully carried out on offset press, by Berto, in Marseille.
    A reprinting of this poster was made in December 1958, but it was made from a typo-lithographic half-tone offset plate, and not from the original zinc.   The result is therefore not half so good as the printing of 1956.   This time the poster is signed by two printers : Berto, in Marseille, and Devaye, in Cannes.

83 TOROS EN VALLAURIS 1957.   Bulls in Vallauris 1957.
    200 prints, 64 × 53 format, and signed by the artist. Original linoleum-cut, Arnera Printers.

84 PEINTURES 1955-1956.   Paintings 1955-1956.   Louise Leiris Gallery, Paris. 1957.
    1,500 prints, 70 × 50 format, original lithograph in three colors, Mourlot Printers.
    25 proofs of this lithograph were printed on Arches vellum for the artist.
    The text was designed by Picasso, after he had turned down several proposals of classical lettering.

85 EXPOSITION VALLAURIS 57.
    175 prints numbered and signed by the artist.   Original linoleum-cut, Arnera Printers.

86 PÂTES BLANCHES.   Whites.   Cannes, August 1957.
    500 prints, 57 × 45 format, offset printing in two colors.

87 MANOLO HUGNET.   Musée d'Art moderne, Céret. August 1957.
    500 prints, 77 × 53 format, original lithograph, Mourlot Printers.
    100 proofs on Arches paper, before lettering, and signed by the artist, who colored some of them with crayon.

PABLO PICASSO (Continued)

88 PÂTES BLANCHES. Whites. Lyons, December 1957.
175 prints, 65 × 50 format, typolithographic printing in two colors, Arnera Printers.

89 PAIX STOCKHOLM. Stockholm Peace. July 1958.
78 × 50 format, printed with text in different languages, Schuster Printers.
Poster produced by photographic offset, from a wax crayon composition.

90 PICASSO – CÉRAMIQUES. Ceramics.
Maison de la Pensée française, Paris. March 1958.
750 prints, 65 × 50 format, original lithograph in three colors, Mourlot Printers.

91 PICASSO – CÉRAMIQUES. Ceramics.
Maison de la Pensée française, Paris. March 1958.
Picasso took out the green in the preceding version.
750 prints, 65 × 50 format, original lithograph in two colors, Mourlot Printers.
200 prints, 160 × 120 format, made from a photographic enlargement of the original lithograph.

92 PICASSO. Musée municipal, Céret. August 1958.
875 prints, and 125 additional prints on Arches paper, and signed by the artist, 65 × 50 format. Original linoleum-cut in two colors, plus the text in blue, Arnera Printers.

93 CÉRAMIQUES – PÂQUES 1958. Ceramics – Easter 1958.
200 prints on vellum offset, and 100 prints, numbered and signed by the artist, 45 × 30 format. Original linoleum-cut, Arnera Printers.

94 TOROS 1958. Bulls 1958.
190 prints, 65 × 53 format, on Arches paper, and signed by the artist. Original linoleum-cut, Arnera Printers.

95 EXPOSITION VALLAURIS 1958.
100 prints on vellum offset, and 175 prints on Arches paper, signed by the artist, 64 × 53 format, three colors, Arnera Printers.

96 VALLAURIS – DIX ANS DE CÉRAMIQUES. Ten years of ceramics. 1958.
1,000 prints, 54 × 33 format, printed in two colors on typolithographic plates, Arnera Printers.

97 HOMMAGE À ANTONIO MACHADO. Tribute to Antonio Machado. Collioure, February 1959.
500 prints, 64 × 46 format, French and Spanish text. Lithographic print in five colors, Mourlot Printers.
A few proofs on Arches paper.

101 LES MENINES. Louise Leiris Gallery, Paris. 1959.
1,500 prints, 66 × 48 format, lithographic print in eight colors from a composition in corresponding size, Mourlot Printers.
Picasso had made a first design for this poster, but he did not use it.

102 AFFICHES ORIGINALES. Original posters.
Maison de la Pensée française, Paris. June 1959.
1,500 prints, 65 × 50 format, original lithograph in three colors, Mourlot Printers.